THE SINGLE MAN'S GUIDE

COOKING WITH BEER

BY:

Streeter F. McClure

Copyright © 2009 SMG Publishing Inc.

ISBN: 9780615232256

Published by SMG Publishing, Denver, Colorado

PRINTED IN THE UNITED STATES OF AMERICA

ALL RIGHTS RESERVED, NO PART OF THIS BOOK MAY BE PRODUCED

WITH OUT SPECIAL PERMISSION FROM THE PUBLISHER

For more Information, please write SMG Publishing, 290 South Forest Street, Denver, CO 80246

Special thanks to Mom, Dad, Melissa, Parker, Robin, Kara, Austin, Clint and Kevin for putting up with me… until the next book!

Mom and me, 2001

DEDICATION PAGE

This book is dedicated, in loving memory, to my mother and friend Elizabeth Ann McClure. It was with her encouragement that my culinary inclinations went from concept to reality. Her spirit lives on through those who were loved and touched by her incredible, indomitable spirit. A portion of the proceeds from the sale of this cookbook will be donated to breast cancer research.

—Streeter F. McClure

FOREWARD

If you mention my name to anyone who knows me, the term 'Culinary God' rarely comes to mind. For years, my repertoire consisted of boxed dinners and ramen noodles. After one particularly long night of debauchery, I opened the fridge and was faced with an onion, a tomato, a leftover cheeseburger and two cans of beer. I was starving, so like many guys in my situation, I decided to toss it all together in a pan with the intent of feeding myself and two ravenous friends. To my complete surprise, it was actually edible.

My life long love of beer, coupled with a desire to impress the ladies, is what inspired me to create a cookbook that single men everywhere could utilize. It is my hope that everyone will be amazed with your incredible ability to incorporate beer into your everyday cooking. They may even be jealous of your new found culinary skills. The girls will love you, the guys will want to be you... Cheers! Bon Appetit!

—Streeter

INTRODUCTION TO THE *SINGLE MAN'S GUIDE*

The Single Man's Guide was written for... The Single Man. The recipes are fun and easy to follow. To assist you in your culinary adventure, the table of contents is set up by category and level of difficulty. The easier recipes appear first within each category. The last recipes are either the most challenging or more time consuming. Please try them all. Crack open a brew and have some fun!

COOKING GEAR FOR THE SINGLE MAN

These items are necessary for the cooking process, many of which can be found on www.thesinglemansguide.com

- serrated knife
- can opener
- cutting board
- bottle opener
- crock pot
- measuring spoons
- wooden spoons
- wire whisk
- measuring cups
- mixing bowls
- grilling tongs
- pot holder
- meat thermometer
- apron
- medium sauce pan

CONTENTS

APPETIZERS
14

General Lee's Wing Ding Wings
Beer Battered Onion Rings
New Orleans Style Crab Cakes
Bacon Wrapped Beer Sausages
Baked Stuffed Mushrooms

SOUP, STEWS AND CHILIES
24

One Beer Chili
Cheese, Beer and Sausage Soup
Brew Stew
Broccoli and Beer Cheese Soup
Irish Stout Stew
White Bean Chicken Chili

SIDES
36

Beer Baked Beans
Gentlemen's Potato Salad
Grilled Veggies
Man Slaw

CONTENTS

BEEF
40

T-Dogs Brisket
Corned Beef, Beer and Cabbage
Street Meat Beer Loaf
No Date Saturday Night Beef Stroganoff
Beer Steak and Chimichurri Sauce

CHICKEN
51

Beer Butt Chicken
Beer Battered Chicken
Kicked Up Chicken Kabobs
Chicken Smothered in Spicy Beer Sauce

FISH
59

Deep Sea Tilapia Tacos
Spring Break Beer Fish
Mom's Lemon Baked Fish
Beer Mussels

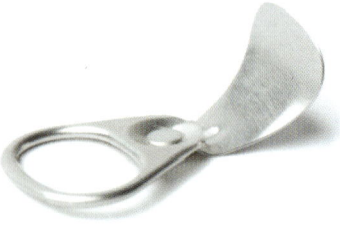

CONTENTS

PORK
66

Beer Brats
Big Bro's Beer Hocks and Beans
Uncle Duke's Beer Glazed Smoked Ham
Spare Ribs in Beer-B-Q Sauce

BREADS
72

Dorm Room Rye Beer Bread
Half Time Beer Bread

BEER GUIDE
76

INDEX
77

GENERAL LEE'S WING DING WINGS

Serves: 2 to 4

Sauce

1 can pilsner
3 whole serrano chili peppers
1C. Red Hot™ sauce
¼ C. worcestershire sauce
1 T. cayenne pepper
1 T. salt
1 T. black ground pepper
¼ cup vinegar
2 T. honey

2 lb Chicken Wings

- In a blender puree all sauce ingredients, except butter
- Marinate wings in sauce
- Put wings in covered bowl, refrigerate overnight
- Place wings on sheet pan, save some sauce to pour over wings later
- Broil on low for 10 - 15 min. or until golden brown
- Transfer remaining marinade to sauce pan
- Bring sauce to boil on medium heat, decrease heat and simmer until sauce is thick
- Add 1 stick butter
- Remove wings from oven, pour thickened sauce over wings to coat them evenly
- Broil another 5 minutes

t. | Teaspoon • T. | Tablespoon • C. | Cup

BEER BATTERED ONION RINGS

Serves: 2 to 4

1 ⅓ C. flour
1 T. seasoning salt
½ t. salt
½ t. white pepper
1 T. melted butter
2 egg yolks
1 bottle brown ale
2 egg whites
2 large yellow onions
3 C. vegetable oil

Batter

- Mix first six ingredients
- Slowly add one bottle of beer, stirring constantly
- Refrigerate for 4 hours

Egg Whites

- Place separated whites in to mixing bowl
- Using electric mixer, beat whites until stiff peaks form

Onions

- Cut off the bottom and tip of the onion, peel away first layer of skin
- Cut desired size rings of onion

Rings

- Cover bottom of frying pan with vegetable oil. Cook oil over medium heat until oil bubbles. Coat each ring with batter, shake off excess. Place rings in pan being sure not to crowd them. When they turn golden brown, remove from heat, drain on to paper towels.

t. | Teaspoon • T. | Tablespoon • C. | Cup

17

NEW ORLEANS STYLE CRAB CAKES

Serves: 2 to 4

1 package Zatarains™ crab cake mix

1 lb crab meat

¼ C. mayonnaise

½ C. wheat beer (room temp)

¼ C. diced red bell pepper

¼ C. diced green onion

2 garlic cloves, minced

2 C. bread crumbs

1 egg

1 t. Tabasco™ sauce

- Combine and thoroughly mix all ingredients in a large bowl
- Allow mixture to set in fridge for 30 minutes
- Form mixture into 10 to 12 separate patties
- Pre-heat in ½ inch of oil on medium heat in large sauce pan
- Fry patties 2 to 3 at a time, browning on each side

t. | Teaspoon • T. | Tablespoon • C. | Cup

BACON WRAPPED BEER SAUSAGES

Serves: 2 to 4

2 bottles pale ale

1 package mini sausages

2 packages center cut bacon

Toothpicks

Pre-heat oven to 350 degrees

- Pour both bottles of ale into saucepan, bring to boil over medium heat
- While bringing to boil, use fork to punch holes in mini sausages
- Add sausages to beer, reduce heat to medium, cook 5 minutes
- Remove from heat and allow to cool

- While sausages are cooling, cut bacon strips in half
- Arrange on microwave safe plate and cook for 20 seconds
- Wrap sausages with a half strip of bacon, using toothpick to hold ends in place
- Bake in oven for 10 to 15 minutes or until bacon is crispy
- Serve with sliced green pepper and sliced red onion

t. | Teaspoon • T. | Tablespoon • C. | Cup

BAKED STUFFED MUSHROOMS

Serves: 2 to 4

1 stick butter

1 small yellow onion, finely chopped

3 T. parmesan cheese

⅓ C. brown ale

½ t. worcestershire sauce

1 C. bread crumbs

1 lb mushrooms (remove caps and chop stems)

½ t. salt

½ t. pepper

½ t. garlic powder

¼ t. chili powder

¼ t. oregano

- Melt butter in sauce pan or in microwave
- Cook chopped onion over medium heat until translucent
- Add chopped mushroom stems to butter and onions
- Stir in bread crumbs, seasoning and cheese
- Add beer, brown all ingredients, stirring often
- Stuff mixture into caps until mixture covers the cap
- Bake at 350 degrees for 15 minutes

t. | Teaspoon • **T.** | Tablespoon • **C.** | Cup

ONE BEER CHILI

Serves: 4 to 6

1 bottle pilsner
2 lb ground beef
1 large white onion, chopped
2 C. water
1 (12 oz) can diced tomatoes
3 (7 oz) cans tomato sauce
2 T. chili powder
1 t. cumin
1 T. salt
1 t. pepper
1 dash cayenne pepper
1 can ranch-style beans

- Brown meat and onion in small pan over medium heat
- Cook meat fully, drain all grease, pour into crock pot
- Add remaining ingredients, cook for 2 hours
- Adjust flavor with salt, pepper and other spices if desired

Too hot... Add 1 to 2 t. sugar

Not hot enough... increase cayenne pepper

t. | Teaspoon • T. | Tablespoon • C. | Cup

CHEESE, BEER AND SAUSAGE SOUP

Serves: 4 to 6

1 bottle pilsner
64 oz chicken stock
1 ham bone
1 white onion, chopped
2 sticks butter
2 C. flour
¾ lb sharp cheddar, cubed
2 C. milk
2 large Kielbasa sausage, pre-cooked, cooled and sliced

- In large pot, simmer stck, ham bone and onion on low heat for one hour
- Strain broth into large bowl or second pot
- Discard ham bone
- In clean pot, melt butter
- Whisk in flour, heat on medium for 5 minutes, stirring constantly
- Add broth to flour mixture 2 cups at a time, continuing to whisk until smooth
- Add cheese, stir until melted
- Add beer and stir
- Add sausage, heat mixture on low until ready to serve
- Salt and pepper to taste

t. | Teaspoon • **T.** | Tablespoon • **C.** | Cup

BREW STEW

Serves: 4 to 6

1 bottle pale ale beer
3 lb boneless beef chuck, cubed into 1 ½ inch pieces
3 T. all purpose flour
4 carrots, chopped
4 stalks celery, chopped
1 white onion, chopped
3 potatoes, cubed
4 garlic cloves, minced
1 C. medium size mushrooms, diced
¼ C. olive oil
2 ½ C. beef broth

- Place beef in large bowl
- Sprinkle with flour
- Salt and pepper generously; toss to coat evenly
- Heat oil in large, heavy pot over medium-heat
- Working in batches, sauteé beef until brown
- Put browned beef in crock-pot
- Add beer, beef broth, carrots, potatoes, onions and chopped garlic
- cover and cook on low heat for 3 hours
- add mushrooms 15 minutes before serving

t. | Teaspoon • T. | Tablespoon • C. | Cup

BROCCOLI AND BEER CHEESE SOUP

Serves: 4 to 6

½ C. butter
1 white onion, chopped
1 (16 oz) package broccoli, chopped
1 (8 oz) package corn, frozen
3 (14.5 oz) cans chicken broth
1 lb Velveeta™, cubed
1 C. milk
½ T. garlic powder
1 t. mustard powder
1 t. chili powder
1 t. black pepper
1 T. corn starch
1 bottle pale ale

- In large pot, over medium heat, melt butter
- Sauteé onion until transparent
- Stir in broccoli and corn, cook for 2 minutes
- Cover with chicken broth, cook for 15 minutes
- Reduce heat, stir in cheese cubes and milk, stirring frequently until cheese is melted
- Add garlic, mustard, chili powder and pepper
- In small bowl, stir cornstarch and slowly add beer until cornstarch is completely dissolved
- Add beer mixture to soup, stirring frequently until soup becomes thick

t. | Teaspoon • T. | Tablespoon • C. | Cup

IRISH STOUT STEW

Serves: 4 to 6

1 bottle stout
32 oz beef broth
2 C. water
1 ½ lb lamb, cubed
2 large yellow onions, chopped
2 large carrots, diced
1 lb red potatoes, chopped
¼ C. fresh parsley, chopped
2 T. fresh thyme, chopped
1 C. fresh spinach
1 T. salt
1 T. pepper

- Place lamb in large bowl
- Sprinkle with salt and pepper, toss to coat
- Heat oil in heavy, large pot over medium-high heat
- Working in batches, add lamb and sauteé until brown
- Pour browned lamb and drippings into crock-pot
- Add beer, water and beef broth
- Toss in carrots and onions, cover and cook over medium heat for 3 hours
- After 3 hours add parsley, fresh thyme and spinach
- Cook an additional hour and serve

WHITE BEAN CHICKEN CHILI

Serves: 4 to 6

Soup
1 lb boneless, skinless chicken breast
1 small onion, diced
2 (15 oz) cans northern beans
2 (14.5 oz) cans chicken broth
2 (4.5 oz) cans chopped green chilies
1 (10.5 oz) can cream of chicken soup
3 T. hot sauce
1 bottle wheat beer

Spices
½ T. cumin
1 T. chile powder
¼ t. white pepper
½ T. garlic powder
salt and pepper to taste

Toppings:
flour tortillas
sour cream
monterrey jack cheese
fresh cilantro

- Sauteé chicken in 1 T. of olive oil until golden brown
- Mix canned ingredients together with cubed chicken in large pot
- Season with salt, white pepper and garlic powder
- Add chile powder and cumin to taste
- Heat soup over medium heat
- Cut tortillas into strips. Line bowl with strips Ladle in chili
- Top with sour cream and monterrey jack cheese
- Garnish with fresh cilantro

t. | Teaspoon • T. | Tablespoon • C. | Cup

BEER BAKED BEANS

Serves: 3 to 5

½ cup amber ale beer
3 strips of bacon
1 small onion
¼ C. red bell pepper, chopped
2 (36 oz) cans of baked beans
2 t. worcestershire sauce
½ t. garlic powder
¼ C. yellow mustard
3 t. hot sauce
½ t. ground pepper
½ t. brown sugar

- Dice onion and pepper, slice raw bacon into bite size pieces
- Cook bacon with diced onion in medium-sized saucepan until bacon is crisp
- Pour in baked beans and mix in amber ale, mustard, worcestershire and hot sauce
- Season with ground pepper and brown sugar
- Heat to a boil, reduce heat and simmer, stirring often until slightly thickened, about 20 minutes

t. | Teaspoon • T. | Tablespoon • C. | Cup

GENTLEMAN'S POTATO SALAD

Serves: 4 to 6

2 lb small new potatoes
2 C. celery chopped
1 small green onion, chopped
1 C. mayonnaise
2 T. dijon mustard
¼ t. red pepper flakes
¼ C. wheat beer
2 T. parsley, chopped
3 small radishes, sliced

- Boil potatoes in skins until tender
- When cool, peel and dice, add celery and onion
- Season to taste with salt
- Blend mayonnaise with mustard and pepper
- Gradually stir in beer, add parsley
- Pour over potato mixture, mix lightly
- Refrigerate for 2 hours
- Garnish with sliced radishes

t. | Teaspoon • **T.** | Tablespoon • **C.** | Cup

GRILLED VEGGIES

Serves: 4 to 6

½ C. lager beer

2 large white onions

3 large green peppers

2 zucchini

2 limes

¼ C. soy sauce

¼ C. olive oil

½ t. ground cumin

½ t. salt

¼ t. ground black pepper

- Slice the onions, green peppers and zucchini into ¼ inch thick pieces
- Light a grill or preheat the broiler
- In a large bowl, combine the lager beer, soy sauce, olive oil, lime juice, onion, cumin, salt and pepper
- Add the onions, green peppers, zucchini slices and toss to coat
- Let stand for up to 20 minutes
- Grill or broil vegetables for about 3 minutes per side, until browned and tender
- Serve hot

t. | Teaspoon • T. | Tablespoon • C. | Cup

MAN SLAW

Serves: 3 to 5

1 medium head green cabbage, shredded
½ medium head red cabbage, shredded
1 carrot, shredded
2 T. minced green onion
½ C. mayonnaise
⅓ C. sugar
¼ C. India Pale Ale
¼ t. celery seed
¼ t. paprika
¼ C. dijon mustard

- Shred cabbage into a large bowl
- Add shredded carrot and onion
- Combine mayonnaise, sugar, beer, celery seed and mustard
- Add salt and pepper to taste
- Toss cabbage mixture with dressing
- Refrigerate for 1 hour

t. | Teaspoon • T. | Tablespoon • C. | Cup

T- DOG'S BRISKET

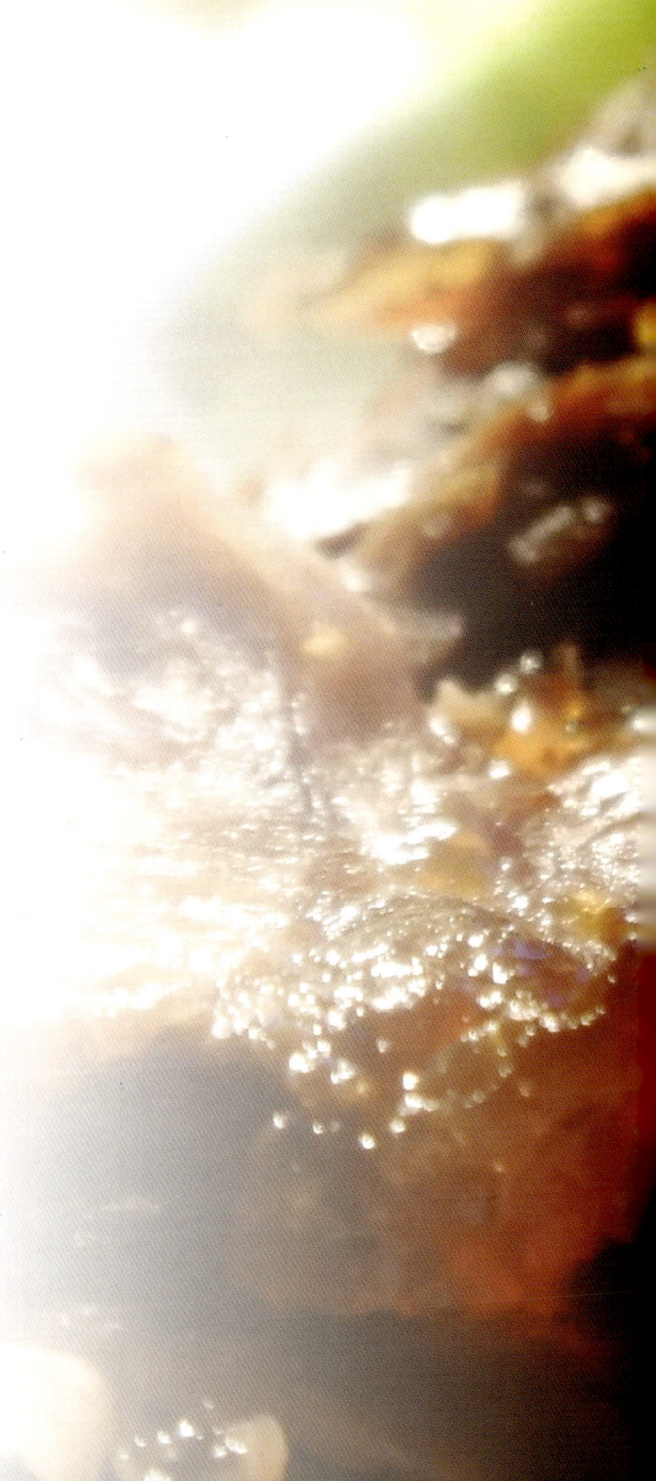

Serves: 4 to 6

1 bottle pilsner

2 lb brisket

1 C. salsa

1 packet onion and mushroom soup mix

2½ T. brown sugar

- Mix beer and salsa in small bowl, set aside
- Lay meat on aluminum foil
- Mix brown sugar and soup mix and rub all over meat
- Pour beer mixture around meat
- Wrap tightly in aluminum foil
- Cook at 250 degrees for 5 to 6 hours
- Slice aluminum across the top and serve

t. | Teaspoon • T. | Tablespoon • C. | Cup

CORNED BEEF, BEER AND CABBAGE

Serves: 4 to 6

1 bottle lager beer

6 C. water

1 packaged prepared corned beef (comes with spice packet)

¾ head of cabbage, roughly chopped

3 large carrots, peeled and diced

1 lb new potatos

½ onion, roughly chopped

1 t. black pepper

2 cloves garlic, minced

- Place corned beef in crock pot on low
- (Or place in deep pan at 300 degrees)
- Add chopped onion, garlic, carrots, potatoes, beer, 6 cups water, pepper and corned beef spice packet
- Cover and cook 4 hours
- After 4 hours, add cabbage
- Cover and cook for 30 minutes

t. | Teaspoon • T. | Tablespoon • C. | Cup

STREET MEAT BEER LOAF

Serves: 3 to 5

¾ bottle amber ale
½ lb ground beef
½ lb bacon
½ lb ground pork
1 green pepper, chopped
1 white onion, chopped
1 cup bread crumbs
1 t. salt
1 t. pepper
½ C. salsa
¼ C. garlic, diced

- Knead beef and pork together
- Cover with beer and salsa
- Add chopped green pepper, onion, breadcrumbs, salt, pepper and garlic, mix

To Cook

- Pre-heat oven to 350 degrees
- Form mixture into loaf, use pre-greased bread pan to shape
- Lay bacon strips over top of loaf
- Bake for 45 minutes

t. | Teaspoon • T. | Tablespoon • C. | Cup

NO DATE SATURDAY NIGHT BEEF STROGANOFF

Serves: 4 to 6

1 bottle porter
2 lb sirloin steak
1 can mushrooms, sliced
12 oz beef stock
1 large white onion, chopped
¼ C. ketchup
2 cloves garlic, chopped
1 t. salt
⅓ C. flour
1 cup sour cream
10 ounce package of egg noodles
3 T. butter

- Cut meat into strips
- In frying pan, brown meat in butter for 5 minutes
- In same pan, add sauteéd mushrooms and onions
- Deglaze pan with beef stock and reduce by half
- Add garlic, ketchup and salt
- Cover and simmer 10 minutes
- Mix beer and flour and slowly add to meat mixture
- Bring to boil, stirring constantly for 1 minute
- Stir in sour cream and heat thoroughly
- Cook and drain noodles as directed
- Serve Stroganoff over noodles

t. | Teaspoon • **T.** | Tablespoon • **C.** | Cup

BEER STEAK AND CHIMICHURRI SAUCE

Serves: 2 to 4

2 lb hangar or flank steak

Sauce

1 ½ C. firmly packed flat leaf parsley, roughly chopped

6 cloves garlic, quartered

2 t. fresh oregano leaves, roughly chopped

¾ C. extra virgin olive oil

¼ t. red pepper flakes

3 T. red wine vinegar

coarse sea salt to taste

Marinade

½ C. soy sauce

1 C. India Pale Ale

- Mix marinade in bowl and pour over steaks, refrigerate for 2 hours
- Combine parsley, vinegar, garlic, oregano, red pepper flakes and salt in food processor
- Pulsate until mixture is combined and parsley and oregano are finely chopped
- While continuing to pulsate mix, slowly add olive oil
- When liquid is fully incorporated, taste for flavor, add more pepper flakes and salt to taste
- Serve over grilled or broiled steak

Chef's tip: "Cut steak against grain."

t. | Teaspoon • T. | Tablespoon • C. | Cup

BEER BUTT CHICKEN

Serves: 3 to 5

1 can pilsner

1 whole chicken

½ stick butter, melted

½ white onion

⅛ C. seasoning salt

⅛ C. sage, rosemary and parsley, diced

- Remove gizzards from body cavity of chicken
- Drink ½ can of beer
- Melt butter with herbs
- Add mixture to remaining ½ can of beer
- Insert onion into chicken cavity then push beer can into chicken
- Fire up grill until coals are red hot
- Rub entire exterior of chicken with seasoning salt, pepper to taste
- Set chicken on grill directly above coals
- Cover and let cook for 1 ½ hours or until chicken reaches internal temperatue of 175 degrees

t. | Teaspoon • **T.** | Tablespoon • **C.** | Cup

BEER BATTERED CHICKEN

Serves: 3 to 5

1 ⅓ C. flour
1 t. seasoning salt
½ t. salt
½ t. white pepper
1 T. melted butter or olive oil
1 t. black pepper
1 bottle brown ale
2 egg yolks, beaten
2 egg whites, stiffly beaten
2 C. vegetable oil (for frying)
1 C. flour (for dredging)

Batter

- Mix first six ingredients
- Add beer to first 6 ingredients
- Slowly stir for 1 minute or until beer is saturated into mixture
- Refrigerate for 4 hours

Egg Whites

- Place separated whites in clean, dry mixing bowl
- Using electric mixer, beat whites on low until stiff peaks form

A stiff peak is the equivalent of a beaten egg white mountain… when you pull the beater up from the mixture a "stiff peak" should be left behind….

- Upon forming stiff peaks, remove batter mixture from fridge
- Gently fold in egg whites to batter
- Coat chicken in dredging flour
- Batter chicken and fry in vegetable oil until golden brown

t. | Teaspoon • T. | Tablespoon • C. | Cup

KICKED UP CHICKEN KABOBS

Serves: 4 to 6

2 lb boneless, skinless chicken breast, cut into small cubes

¼ C. wheat beer

¼ C. dijon mustard

¼ C. olive oil

1 t. dried or fresh dill

2 t. hot sauce

1 green pepper, cut into pieces

1 zucchini cut into small rounds

1 onion cut into cube-shaped pieces

1 package wooden skewers, soaked for 20 minutes in water

- Place cubed chicken into doubled up large ziplock bags
- Add beer, mustard, olive oil, dill, hot sauce and salt and pepper to chicken
- Marinate for at least 20 minutes in the fridge
- Meanwhile… cut vegetables into kabob size pieces and soak wooden skewers in baking dish filled with water
- Remove chicken from fridge and thread on skewers alternating with vegetables
- Cook on grill until nicely charred
- Alternate cooking method; pre-heat oven to 350 degrees
- Cook chicken kabobs in a sheet pan in the oven for 10 minutes on each side, turning once

t. | Teaspoon • **T.** | Tablespoon • **C.** | Cup

CHICKEN SMOTHERED IN SPICY BEER SAUCE

Serves: 2 to 4

½ bottle amber ale

2 boneless, skinless chicken breasts

⅓ C. italian dressing

⅛ t. pepper

1 T. dijon mustard

½ C. heavy whipping cream

2 t. Tabasco™ sauce

1 t. salt

- In frying pan, heat Italian dressing over medium heat
- Place chicken breasts in pan and fry in Italian dressing until golden brown (using a lid will lock in moisture and cook the breast thoroughly)
- Remove lid after 10 to 15 minutes and cook for an additional 2 minutes
- Remove chicken from pan, add beer, salt, pepper and mustard, bring to boil
- Reduce heat and simmer 8 minutes, stirring occasionally, add cream and Tabasco™ sauce
- Cook 1 minute until thickened, pour over chicken, and serve

t. | Teaspoon • T. | Tablespoon • C. | Cup

DEEP SEA TILAPIA TACOS

Serves: 3 to 5

1 bottle lager
1 Can chipotle chilies and adobo sauce
¼ C. honey
1 T. garlic salt
½ T. pepper
juice of ½ lime

½ lb (per person) tilapia or other white flakey fish
(sole is a great option… ask your local supermarket sea food manager if you can't find tilapia or sole)

1 package small white corn tortillas
sour cream

Single Man's Slaw (see recipe page 39)

- Remove Chiles from Adobo Sauce and set aside
- Combine beer, 2 T. adobo sauce, 2 chipotle chilies, honey, garlic salt, pepper and juice of lime in blender and puree until smooth
- Place fish fillets in large Ziploc bag and add marinade to bag
- Refrigerate for 1 hour
- Line heavy baking dish with foil and spray with non-stick cooking spray
- Carefully place fish and marinade on baking pan, reserving half of marinade to use while cooking
- Bake at 350 degrees for 15 minutes
- Turn oven to high broil, add remaining marinade, broil 5 to 10 minutes or until crispy
- Serve fish in white corn tortillas with Single Man's Slaw and sour cream

t. | Teaspoon • **T.** | Tablespoon • **C.** | Cup

SPRING BREAK BEER FISH

Serves: 3 to 5

½ bottle brown ale

juice of 1 lime

¼ C. soy sauce

¼ C. maple syrup

½ C. fresh ginger, roughly chopped

3 cloves garlic, roughly chopped

1 t. red pepper flake

½ lb salmon fillets (per person)

- Thaw fish if frozen (run under cool water for 20 minutes)
- Mix all ingredients in bowl
- Marinate fish in large Ziploc bag for 1 hour
- Bake uncovered at 450 degrees, until fish flakes easily when tested with a fork
- Cook about 5 minutes for each half inch of thickness

This dish can easily be made in a foil pouch on the grill... A simple foil tent will seal in the juices and leave you free to watch the game without burning your dinner

t. | Teaspoon • T. | Tablespoon • C. | Cup

MOM'S LEMON BAKED FISH

Serves: 4 to 6

½ bottle of light lager

3 to 4 fillets of trout, haddock or cod

2 lemons

2 cloves garlic, dliced

¼ C. bread crumbs

1 T. parsley

salt and pepper

- Pre-heat oven to 375 degrees
- Place sheet of foil on baking pan, ban
- Brush sheet of foil with olive oil an
- Pour ½ bottle of beer over fillets
- Sprinkle salt, pepper, diced ga ts
- Squeeze juice of lemon over f
- Wrap foil to form cooking p
- Open foil pouch and broil are crispy and brown
- Remove fish from foil pac

t. | Teaspoon • **T.** | Tablespoon • **C.** | Cup

BEER MUSSELS

Serves: 3 to 5

2 lb cleaned Pei Mussels (cleaned and de-bearded)
1 lb sausage
2 slices of thick cut bacon, cut into ½" pieces
2 celery stalks
1 large carrot
1 leek
4 cloves garlic, minced
1 can (24 ounces) stewed whole tomatoes, drained and chopped
¼ C. basil, cut into small pieces
1 T. olive oil
1 bottle of pilsner beer
2 T. butter
salt and pepper to taste

- Place a large, empty, oven proof pot in pre-heated oven to 325 degrees
- Cut carrot and celery into ¼" cubes and set aside
- Using only the bottom half of the leek, cut in half slicing thinly, set aside
- In large sauteé pan heat olive oil on medium low heat
- Brown the sausage and bacon over medium low heat, breaking up the sausage into smaller pieces
- Remove sausage and bacon from the pan and drain on to paper towels
- Add the carrots, celery and leek to the pan and sauteé in oil from bacon and sasage over low heat for 10 minutes, stirring frequently
- Add chopped tomatoes to pan with vegetables, and the basil
- Continue cooking over medium low heat until most of the moisture is cooked out, season to taste
- Remove pot from the preheated oven and add the tomato mixture to it, followed by the mussels, beer and then sausage add bacon right on top
- Cover the pot with a lid and return to oven for 5 minutes or until the mussels have opened up
- Stir butter into the contents of the pot, serve

t. | Teaspoon • T. | Tablespoon • C. | Cup

BEER BRATS

Serves: 2 to 4

2 bottles of pale ale
1 package of bratwurst links
½ white onion, diced
½ green bell pepper, diced
½ red bell pepper, diced
½ C. of jalapenos, diced
1 package of hot dog buns
¼ stick of butter

- Fire up the grill. Pour both bottles of beer into a saucepan
- Bring to a boil
- Add links to the beer, reduce heat to medium and cook links for 8 minutes
- Grill or bake bratwurst until the center is no longer pink

Pepper Medly

- While bratwursts are cooking, melt butter over medium heat
- Add diced green pepper, white onion, jalapenos and red pepper
- Sauteé veggies until onions are golden brown, then reduce the heat to low.
- Serve links in buns smothered with the pepper medley

BIG BRO'S BEER HOCKS & BEANS

Serves: 3 to 5

1 bottle pilsner beer

4 smoked ham hocks (ask for them in the meat department)

36 oz of beef broth

6 C. water

3 large carrots

3 stalks of celery, chopped

1 lb bag of black beans, uncooked

4 cloves garlic, chopped

1 white onion, chopped

- Place the ham hocks in a crock-pot or pan over low heat
- Pour beer, beef broth and 6 cups of water into pan/crock pot
- Add beans, cover and let cook for 2 hours, stirring occasionally
- Add roughly chopped garlic, onions, celery and carrots
- Cover and cook an additional 2 hours, stirring occasionally

UNCLE DUKE'S BEER GLAZED SMOKED HAM

Serves: 4 to 6

1 bottle porter

1 spiral cut ham (6 to 10 lb)

½ C. brown sugar

1 t. liquid smoke

¼ C. yellow mustard

- Light coals on one side of grill
- When coals are red, place wet stick of smoke flavored wood over coals
- Place ham in a pan on the other end of the grill
- Be sure to open grill slits at both ends to create smoke current
- In medium bowl, combine beer, brown sugar, liquid smoke and yellow mustard
- Baste ham with sauce every 30 minutes
- Check wood and add more if necessary
- Smoke for 4 to 6 hours

SPARE RIBS IN BEER-B-Q SAUCE

Serves: 2 to 4

¼ bottle brown ale

12-16 spare ribs

1 T. flour

¼ can cola

½ C. BBQ sauce

¼ C. Tabasco™ sauce

1 t. liquid smoke

- In bowl, mix beer, cola, flour, BBQ sauce and hot sauce
- Marinate ribs in sauce overnight in refrigerator
- Pre-heat oven to 425 degrees or heat grill to high
- Place ribs in foil bag and cover with half of marinade
- Place foil bag in oven or on grill and cook for 1 hour
- Remove and serve with remaining sauce

DORM ROOM RYE BEER BREAD

Serves: 2 to 4

1 ½ bottle lager
½ C. warm water
2 t. salt
½ C. molasses
2 packages active yeast
5 T. vegetable shortening
3 ½ C. all purpose flour
3 ¼ C. rye flour

- Pre-heat oven to 375 degrees
- In medium bowl, mix beer, water, salt, molasses, yeast and vegetable shortening
- Let mixture set 25 minutes
- Add both flours to bowl and stir until dough forms solid mass
- Place dough on floured surface and knead for 10 minutes
- Place dough in dry clean bowl, cover bowl with damp paper towel , let rise for 1 hour
- Return to work surface, cut dough into two equal pieces, shape in round, greased loaf pans
- Cover pans with damp cloth, allow to rise 1 additional hour
- Brush the top of dough with slightly beaten egg
- Bake 40 minutes at 375 degrees
- Remove and cool 30 minutes

HALF TIME BEER BREAD

Serves: 2 to 4

- 1 bottle lager
- 3 C. all purpose flour
- 5 t. baking powder
- 1 t. salt
- 3 ½ T. sugar

- Pre-heat oven to 400 degrees, grease loaf pan
- Combine ingredients in bowl, mix well
- Transfer batter into greased pan
- Bake at 400 degrees for 1 hour

t. | Teaspoon • T. | Tablespoon • C. | Cup

STREETER'S BUCKET O' BEER

Serves: Friends

- 1 Bucket
- 1 Bag of Ice
- 1 Case of Bottled Beer
- Serve your closest buddies

Beer, with its extensive variety of blends and flavors, lends itself as an exceptional ingredient for cooking. I have found that as a rule, the less bitter the beer, the better it is for cooking. A pinch of sugar or salt can help alter the way a beer tastes, making it a liquid that is easy to manipulate. Use creativity when you pair beer with a meal you are serving. If you are hungry for a hearty meal, grab yourself a chilled beer and start cooking. Remember to taste as you cook and drink while you are cooking. Some of my best work was discovered several drinks in. Add your own twist to the recipes as you see fit. There's a perfect beer for just about any main dish, as long as you match the intensity of the beer to the food. Now, grab an apron, your favorite 6 pack and get to work! The Beer Pairing Chart will not only help you learn your beers, but assist you in paring beer with any meal.

t. | Teaspoon • T. | Tablespoon • C. | Cup

BEER PAIRING CHART

Legend: Alcohol | Flavor Impact | Color | Bitterness

Color approximates actual beer
Shaded circles = range of variation

Alcohol/volume: 3% – 10%+
Hop Bitterness: 15 IBU – 70+
Flavor impact: Delicate – Intense

Beer Type		Suggested Foods	Cheese	Dessert	Serving Temp
1. Kölsch, Cream Ale, Blonde Ale		Lighter food: chicken, salads, salmon, bratwurst; Monterey jack cheese	Monterey Jack, Brick or similar light nutty cheese	Light apricot or mandarin cake, or lemon custard tart	4.5–7 C / 40–45 F
2. British-Style Bitter		Wide range of food: try roast chicken or pork, fish & chips; mild cheese	Mild English cheese such as Lancashire or Leicester	Oatmeal-raisin-walnut cookies or some other satisfyingly basic dish	10–13 C / 50–55 F
3. Pale Ale		Wide range of food: meat pie, English cheese; great with a burger!	English cheese such as Cheddar or Derby with sage	Pumpkin flan, maple bread pudding, bananas Foster	10–13 C / 50–55 F
4. India Pale Ale		Strong, spicy food (classic with curry!) bold, sweet desserts like carrot cake	Milder blue such as Gorgonzola or Cambozola	Caramel apple tart, ginger spice cake, persimmon rice pudding	10–13 C / 50–55 F
5. Double/Imperial IPA		Smoked beef brisket, grilled lamb; Southern chicken-fried steak	Sharp and rich American artisanal blue	Very sweet desserts like carrot cake, caramel cheesecake or crème brûlée	10–13 C / 50–55 F
6. Amber/Red Ale		Wide range of food: chicken, seafood, burgers; great with spicy cuisine	Port-Salut or other lightly tangy cheese	Poached pears with dulce de leche, banana pound cake, pecan lace cookies	10–13 C / 50–55 F
7. Scotch Ale/Wee Heavy		Roasted or grilled beef, lamb, game, smoked salmon	Aged sheep cheese: Mizithra or Idiazabal (smoked!)	Brilliant with sticky toffee pudding or chocolate chip shortbread	10–13 C / 50–55 F
8. Brown Ale, Altbier		Hearty foods: roast pork, smoked sausage, grilled salmon	Aged Gouda or a crumbly Cheshire	Almond or maple-walnut cake, pear fritters, cashew brittle	10–13 C / 50–55 F
9. Abbey Dubbel		Barbecue, meat stews, or a nice thick steak or roast rib roast	Washed-rind abbey-type cheese or French Morbier	Heavenly with milk chocolate: butter truffles, chocolate bread pudding	10–13 C / 50–55 F
10. Abbey Tripel, Strong Golden Ale		Spicy Cajun food, crab cakes, pheasant or roast turkey	Triple-crème such as St. Andre or Explorateur	Non-chocolate desserts: Apricot amaretto tart, baklava, Linzer torte	4.5–7 C / 40–45 F
11. Old or Strong Ale		Big intense dishes such as roast beef, lamb or game, grilled or roasted	Double Gloucester or other rich moderately-aged cheese.	Spiced plum-walnut tart, classic canolli, toffee apple crisp	10–13 C / 50–55 F
12. Barley Wine		Easily overpowers most main dishes. Best with strong cheese or dessert	Stilton and walnuts is a classic updated. Who needs Port?	Rich, sweet desserts: chocolate hazelnut torte, toffee caramel cheesecake	10–13 C / 50–55 F
13. Porter		Roasted or smoked food: barbecue, sausages, roast meat, blackened fish	Cow milk such as Tilsit or Gruyère.	Chocolate peanut butter cookies, toasted coconut cookie bars	10–13 C / 50–55 F
14. Dry Stout		Hearty, rich food: steak, meat pie; a classic with raw oysters.	Irish-type cheese like a Dubliner cheddar.	Chocolate soufflé, tiramisu, mocha mascarpone mousse.	10–13 C / 50–55 F
15. Sweet or Oatmeal Stout		Rich, spicy food like barbecued beef, Oaxacan mole or hearty Szechuan dishes.	Great with very buttery wellaged cheddar	Chocolate espresso cake, cream puffs, profiteroles.	10–13 C / 50–55 F
16. Imperial Stout		Easily overpowers most main dishes, but stands up to foie gras, smoked goose.	Long-aged cheese: Gouda, Parmesan or Cheddar.	Dark chocolate truffles, chocolate raspberry mousse cake.	10–13 C / 50–55 F
17. Hefeweizen		Great with lighter food: salads, seafood, sushi; classic w/weisswurst	Simple chèvre goat cheese or herbed spread such as Boursin.	Strawberry shortcake, fruit trifle or other very light dessert; key lime pie	4.5–7 C / 40–45 F
18. American Wheat Ale		Best with very light foods: salads, sushi, vegetable dishes	Buffalo Mozzarella or Wisconsin Brick.	Generally too light for dessert, but could pair with fresh berries or a fruit soup.	4.5–7 C / 40–45 F
19. Witbier		Great with lighter seafood dishes – classic with steamed mussels.	Mascarpone or herb cheese spread on crackers.	Banana orange crêpes, blood orange sorbet, panna cotta with lemon	4.5–7 C / 40–45 F
20. Dunkelweizen		Substantial salads; roast chicken or pork; excellent with hearty sausage.	Try soft-ripened goat or smoked Gouda.	Sweet potato tart, peach pecan strudel, banana cream pie	7–10 C / 45–50 F
21. Weizenbock		Roast pork, beef, smoked ham or game dishes.	Aged Provolone or Spanish Manchego	Tarte tatin (caramelized apple), pine nut torta with dried fruit, banana soufflée	7–10 C / 45–50 F
22. Classic Pilsener		Great with lighter food: chicken, salads, salmon, bratwurst	A mild white Vermont cheddar	Light desserts: lemon shortbread, fresh berries with sabayon	4.5–7 C / 40–45 F
23. Helles, Dortmunder		Lighter food: salads, seafood, pork; Works with spicy Asian, Cajun, Latin	Wisconsin butterkäse or other soft and mild cheese	Light desserts: blueberry trifle, cranberry apple cobbler	4.5–7 C / 40–45 F
24. Oktoberfest, Märzen, Vienna		Mexican, or any hearty spicy food; chicken, sausage, pork	The perfect beer for spicy Jalapeño Jack	Mango or coconut flan, almond biscotti, spice cake with pine nuts	7–10 C / 45–50 F
25. Amber Lager		Hearty, spicy food: barbecue, hamburgers, chili	White cheddar, jack, brick	Passionfruit bread pudding, pears poached in doppelbock	7–10 C / 45–50 F
26. Dark Lager, Dunkel, Schwarzbier		Hearty, spicy food: barbecue, sausages, roast meat	Authentic washed rind Münster	Pomegranate tart with walnuts, candied ginger pear cake	7–10 C / 45–50 F
27. Maibock/Pale Bock		Spicy food like Thai or Korean Barbecue; great with fried chicken, too	Classic Emmenthal Swiss cheese	Apple almond strudel, white chocolate cheesecake, honey-walnut soufflée	7–10 C / 45–50 F
28. Doppelbock		Rich roasty foods like duck or roasted pork shanks; great with cured meats	Limburger is a classic	German chocolate cake, Black Forest cake, dried fruit (romertopf) rum tart	7–10 C / 45–50 F

Brewers Association
736 Pearl Street, Boulder, CO 80302
(303) 447-0816
www.beertown.org

This is the intellectual property of the Brewers Association. This material was developed by and is the property of the Brewers Association. This can not be reproduced without the permission of the Brewers Association.

INDEX

Appetizers
  Bacon Wrapped Beer Sausages 20
  Baked Stuffed Mushrooms 23
  Beer Battered Onion Rings 17
  General Lee's Wing Ding Wings 14
  New Orleans Style Crab Cakes 18

Beef
  Beer Steak and Chimichurri Sauce 48
  Brew Stew 28
  Corned Beef, Beer and Cabbage 43
  No Date Saturday Night Beef Stroganoff 47
  One Beer Chili 24
  T-Dogs Brisket 40
  Street Meat Beer Loaf 44

Beer
  Amber Ale 36, 44, 56
  Brown Ale 17, 23, 52, 60, 71
  India Pale Ale 39, 48
  Lager 38, 43, 59, 72, 73
  Light Lager 63
  Pale Ale 20, 28, 31, 66
  Pilsner 14, 24, 27, 40, 51, 64, 67
  Porter 47, 68
  Stout 32
  Wheat Beer 18, 35, 37, 55

Beer Guide
  76

Breads
  Dorm Room Rye Beer Bread 72
  Half-Time Beer Bread 73

Chicken
  Beer Battered Chicken 52
  Beer Butt Chicken 51
  Chicken Smothered in Spicy Beer Sauce 56
  Kicked Up Chicken Kabobs 55

Chili
  One Beer Chili 24
  White Bean Chicken Chili 35

Fish
  Beer Mussels 64
  Deep Sea Tilapia Tacos 59
  Mom's Lemon Baked Fish 63
  Spring Break Beer Fish 60

Lamb
  Irish Stout Stew 32

Pork
  Beer Brats 66
  Big Bro's Beer Hocks and Beans 67
  Spare Ribs in Beer-B-Q Sauce 71
  Uncle Duke's Beer Glazed Smoked Ham 68

Sides
  Beer Baked Beans 36
  Gentlemen's Potato Salad 37
  Grilled Veggies 38
  Man Slaw 39

Soup
  Broccoli and Beer Cheese Soup 31
  Cheese, Beer and Sausage Soup 27

Stews
  Brew Stew 28
  Irish Stout Stew 32

Please visit us at
www.thesinglemansguide.com